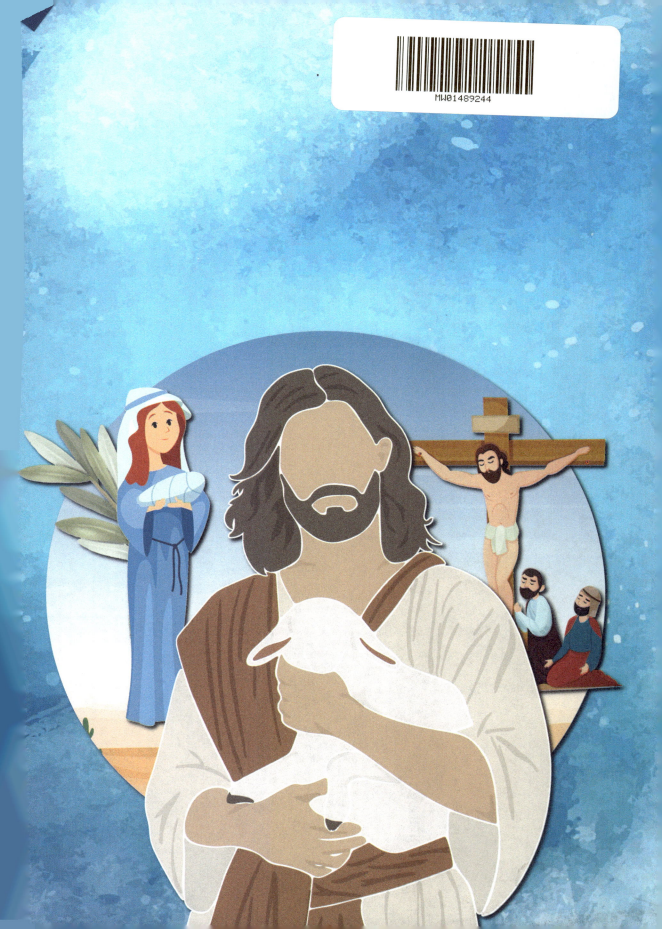

PREAMBLE

This story took place over 2000 years ago in the Near East.

At that time, the regions of Galilee, Judea and Samaria were occupied by the Roman Empire.

THE BIRTH OF JESUS

Mary was a young woman from Nazareth. She was kind and pure. She was engaged to Joseph, a carpenter.

One day, God sent the angel Gabriel to Mary. The angel said to Mary, "You will have a child and you will name him Jesus. He will be the son of God."

God put life into Mary's belly, and she became pregnant.

A few months later, the Roman Emperor Caesar Augustus ordered everyone to go to the city of his ancestors for a census.

Mary and Joseph set out for Bethlehem. When they arrived after a long journey, it was already late and they could not find a place to sleep. So Mary and Joseph settled down in a stable. And that night, surrounded by the animals in the stable, Mary gave birth to Jesus.

THE WISE MEN

On the night of Jesus' birth, a star appeared in the sky above Bethlehem. It was the star of the Nativity (Also called the star of Bethlehem).

Three wise men saw it. For them, it was a sign that a king had been born. So, guided by the star, they went to Bethlehem.

When they arrived, they found Jesus, surrounded by Mary and Joseph.

The Magi knelt before the child.

The first, Melchior, offered gold, the symbol of royalty.

The second, Caspar, offered incense, symbol of divinity.

The third, Balthazar, offered myrrh, symbol of mortality.

THE CHILDHOOD OF JESUS

King Herod heard about the birth of Jesus. He feared that this child would steal his throne. So he sent soldiers to Bethlehem to kill the newborns.

But Joseph had been warned by a dream, and he went to Egypt with Jesus and Mary.

Later, when Herod died, Mary, Jesus, and Joseph returned to Nazareth. Jesus spent his childhood there.

Jesus' family went to Jerusalem every year for Easter.

One day, when he was 12 years old, Jesus went to the temple, where he had a long talk with the priests. They were all surprised by his intelligence.

Later, Jesus became a carpenter, like Joseph.

THE BAPTISM OF JESUS

At the age of 30, Jesus was ready to fulfill his mission.

He asked John the Baptist to baptize him in the Jordan River.

At that moment, the Holy Spirit descended from heaven in the form of a dove, and the voice of God was heard: "You are my beloved son, and in you I have put all my affection."

THE TEMPTATION OF CHRIST

After his baptism, Jesus went to the desert to meditate. He meditated and prayed without ceasing, without eating anything.

After 40 days, Satan approached him and proposed this:

"I can turn stones into bread, to appease your hunger." Jesus refused.

"You can throw yourself from the top of the temple in Jerusalem, to see if God protects you and holds your fall." Jesus refused.

"If you bow down to me, I offer you power over all the kingdoms of the world." Jesus refused again.

Then the devil went away, and Jesus left the desert.

THE MIRACULOUS CATCH OF FISH

Jesus began his journey.

One day, on the shore of Lake Gennesaret, Jesus met Peter (also called Simon), James and John, who were three fishermen.

They had just returned from fishing and had caught no fish.

Then Jesus pointed to a place and said to them, "Cast your nets here."

They cast their nets and brought in a large quantity of fish.

So the three men decided to follow Jesus.

THE DISCIPLES OF JESUS

Jesus continued his journey and asked other men to follow him. These men became his disciples. Jesus called them "the 12 apostles."

There was :
Peter (whose name was really Simon)
Andrew
James (son of Zebedee)
John
Philip
Bartholomew (also called Nathanael)
Thomas
Matthew (also called Levi)
James (son of Alphaeus)
Jude (also called Thaddaeus)
Simon
Judas

THE CHRIST

Jesus began to teach his disciples.

With them, he traveled throughout the country, stopping in towns and villages to teach the Word of God.

One day Jesus asked his disciples, "Who am I to you?"

Peter answered, "You are the Christ, the Son of God."

In Hebrew, "Christ" means the "Messiah," the savior sent by God.

JESUS CLEANSES THE TEMPLE

On his journey, Jesus passed through Jerusalem for Easter.

There he discovered that merchants had set up shop in the temple.

They had even brought in animals and were selling them to passers-by.

Jesus became angry at this sight. He took a rope and beat some of the merchants.

Jesus said to them, "You are here in my Father's house, and you are making it a place of trade. Are you not ashamed?"

Jesus drove them out of the temple.

THE SAMARITAN WOMAN

Jesus was resting near a well in Samaria. His disciples had gone to get something to eat.

A woman came along and Jesus said to her, "If you drink the water from this well, you will always be thirsty. The water I can give you will make you live forever."

The Samaritan woman, was surprised that Jesus, who was a Jew, would speak to her. The Jews hated the Samaritans.

The woman said to him, "Give me some of that water."

Jesus said to her, "The water I am talking about is not the water you drink. I am talking about the Living Water. It is knowledge and truth, it is the Word of God, and it must be shared with everyone."

When Jesus' disciples returned, they were surprised to see Jesus talking to a Samaritan woman.

Jesus said to them, "Let us beware of thinking that some people are evil."

THE SERMON ON THE MOUNT

Jesus gathered his disciples on a mountain near Lake Tiberias.

Jesus told his disciples that he was the son and fulfillment of God.

He taught them forgiveness and sharing, and taught them to pray by reciting the "Our Father" prayer.

Our Father, who art in heaven,
hallowed be thy name,
thy kingdom come,
thy will be done on earth as it is in heaven.

Give us this day our daily bread.

Forgive us our trespasses
as we forgive those who trespass against us.

And lead us not into temptation
but deliver us from evil.

Amen

THE MIRACLES OF JESUS

Jesus performed many miracles during his life. Here are the most famous ones.

Water turned into wine

Jesus went to Cana, a town in Galilee, to attend a wedding. There was not enough wine for all the guests. Mary was there too. She explained the situation to Jesus.

So Jesus took six large amphorae filled with water, and turned the water into wine.

The Healing in Capernaum

In the town of Capernaum, Jesus was teaching. A man came up to him and said, "What are you doing here, Jesus of Nazareth? You have come to lose us!"

The man was aggressive and possessed.

Jesus said to him, "Be quiet and get out of this man!"

Then an unclean spirit came out of the man's body and cried out before disappearing.

The healing of a paralyzed man

Jesus was teaching a crowd of people when some men arrived carrying a paralyzed man.

Jesus came to the man and said, "Get up and walk."

In front of the astonished crowd, the man got up, walked and went home.

The Healing of a Blind Man

As Jesus was leaving the city of Jericho, he met a blind beggar named Bartimaeus.

The blind man said "Jesus, have mercy on me."

Jesus came up to him and asked, "What do you want me to do for you? ". Bartimaeus replied, "I want to see again."

Jesus told him that he was healed. Bartimaeus opened his eyes and could see Jesus' face.

The multiplication of the loaves

Jesus was now followed by a crowd of more than 5000 people.

One evening, there was almost nothing left to eat, only 5 loaves and 2 fish.

The apostles were worried and went to tell Jesus.

Jesus began to pray and the loaves multiplied so much that everyone had enough to eat.

Jesus walks on water

Jesus and his disciples were to take a boat on their journey. Jesus said to them, "Get in the boat and go, I'll stay here to pray and then I'll join you."

The disciples then got into the boat, which left the shore.

Later, they saw a human form approaching the boat. They thought they saw a ghost and then recognized Jesus.

Fearing for Jesus, Peter jumped into the water to join him, but began to sink. Jesus came to him, walking on the water, and then grabbed him to bring him back to the boat.

The daughter of Jairus

A man named Jairus came to Jesus and said, "My only daughter is sick and dying. Come and save her."

Jesus agreed and set out on his journey, accompanied by the apostles and a crowd. On the way, a sick woman touched Jesus' cloak and was healed immediately.

Jairus regained hope for his daughter, but a messenger arrived and told him, "Your daughter is dead." Jesus told him not to worry and went on his way.

When he reached the house, Jesus took the girl's hand and said, "Get up." So the girl got up and walked, alive and healed.

The calming of a storm

One evening when Jesus and his apostles were in a boat, a storm arose.

The waves were so high that the boat filled with water. The disciples became afraid and thought they were going to die.

Jesus got up and ordered the storm to stop. Then the wind died down and the waves disappeared.

The healing of the lepers

Jesus was on his way to Jerusalem when he met some lepers. They said to Jesus, "Jesus, have mercy on us."

Jesus replied, "Go on your way and see a priest." As the lepers went their way, they were healed.

The resurrection of Nain.

When Jesus arrived in Nain, he heard that a widow had just lost her young son.

Jesus approached the child and ordered him to get up. The child stood up and began to speak.

The healing of a centurion's servant

A centurion had a servant who was sick and dying. He asked some people to go to Jesus.

Jesus came and the centurion said to him, "Lord, I am not worthy of you, nor do I deserve to have you in my house. That is why I sent these people to find you rather than come in person. But say one word and my servant will be healed."

Jesus said, "You have great faith; your servant will live." When the centurion returned home, his servant was healed.

Healing of Peter's mother-in-law

One day Jesus went to Peter's house. His mother-in -law was sick, lying in bed with a terrible fever.

So Jesus went to her and touched her hand. The fever disappeared at once.

The mother-in-law got up and served them a meal.

The Resurrection of Lazarus

Jesus heard that Lazarus, one of his friends, was seriously ill. He went to the town where Lazarus lived, but when he arrived, his friend had been dead for four days.

Jesus went to the tomb of Lazarus and commanded him to come back to life.

Lazarus rose from the dead, got up, and walked out of his tomb.

The healing of two blind men

One day, when they heard that Jesus was in the area, two blind men went to meet him and said, "Jesus, heal us, we beg you!"

Jesus came to them and said, "Do you believe that I have the power to heal?"

The two blind men answered "yes" and knelt down.

Then Jesus touched their faces and they were healed.

The coin in the fish's mouth

One day, Jesus and Peter were in Capernaum. As they entered the temple, a tax collector came up to them and said, "Don't you and your master pay the temple tax?"

Then Jesus said to Peter, "Go catch a fish in the sea. Open its mouth and you will find a silver coin. Pay our tax with it."

Peter went fishing, and immediately caught a fish. He found a coin in its mouth.

The withered fig tree

One day when Jesus was hungry, he saw a fig tree in the distance. He went up to it but the fig tree had no figs. So Jesus said to the fig tree, "You will never have any fruit!" And the fig tree dried up instantly.

Jesus' disciples asked, "How is it possible that the fig tree dried up?"

Jesus answered, "Have faith and do not doubt. Whatever you ask for with faith through prayer will be granted to you."

The transfiguration of Jesus

Jesus asked Peter, James and John to follow him up a high mountain.

Suddenly, Jesus' face shone like the sun and his clothes became white as light.

The prophets Moses and Elijah appeared from the beyond and spoke with Jesus.

Jesus went around the country for several years, teaching the Word of God, performing miracles and healing the sick.

Many people admired Jesus and paid tribute to him wherever he went.

MARY MAGDALENE

Mary Magdalene (also called Mary of Magdala) was a prostitute from the town of Bethany.

While Jesus was visiting the town, she came to him and fell at his feet, weeping, confessing her sins.

Jesus forgave her and Mary Magdalene became one of his most faithful disciples.

THE FATE OF JESUS

Shortly before Easter, Jesus, now 33 years old, entered Jerusalem, sitting on a donkey and accompanied by his disciples.

The crowd cheered him and placed palm branches on his path.

Jesus went to the temple and healed some blind and sick people.

But the priests and religious leaders did not like Jesus. Maybe they were afraid of him and his miracles? Maybe they were jealous?

Jesus condemned the enrichment of the priests and believed that the only tribute to be paid to God was spiritual.

While the religious leaders conspired against him, Jesus knew that he would soon have to make the sacrifice of his life.

THE LAST MEAL OF CHRIST

Jesus celebrated the Easter meal with his disciples in Jerusalem.

Jesus took bread and broke it, then said, "Eat, this is my body which is given for you."

Then Jesus took a cup of wine and said, "Drink, this is my blood which will be poured out so that the sins of men may be forgiven."

Then Jesus told his disciples to be courageous.

JESUS WASHES THE FEET OF HIS APOSTLES

After the meal, Jesus got up, filled a basin with water, and began to wash the feet of his apostles.

By this symbolic act, Jesus was cleansing his apostles.

Peter refused and said "You are my Master! You will not wash my feet!"

Jesus replied, "The master is not greater than the servant. Follow my example and wash the feet of those who need to be cleansed."

THE BETRAYAL OF JUDAS

After the Easter meal, Jesus went to the Gethsemane area, accompanied by Peter, Andrew, John, and James.

Jesus asked his disciples to sit down and went to pray.

After his prayer, he returned to them and said, "The time has come for the Son of Man to be betrayed."

Judas, one of the 12 apostles, arrived with a group of armed men.

Judas kissed Jesus, in order to point him out to the men who had come to arrest him. Judas had betrayed Jesus for 30 silver coins.

Peter drew his sword and struck a soldier in the ear. Jesus ordered Peter to put away his weapon and touched the soldier's ear to heal him. Jesus was arrested and taken away.

THE CONDEMNATION OF JESUS

Jesus was interrogated by religious leaders.

He was accused of conspiring against the government and leading a rebellion.

The next morning, a Friday, Jesus was taken to Pontius Pilate, the prefect of Judea.

Pontius Pilate did not want to condemn Jesus, but gave in to the pressure of the religious leaders.

The tradition was that a prisoner would be pardoned for Easter.

Then Pontius Pilate asked the crowd which prisoner should be released, giving them the choice between Jesus and Barabbas, a murderer.

The crowd, influenced by the priests, asked that Barabbas be set free.

Jesus was then sentenced to death.

THE PASSION OF THE CHRIST

Jesus was condemned to be crucified the same day.

He was whipped, then the soldiers stripped him of his clothes, placed a crown of thorns on his head, and forced him to carry his cross to Mount Golgotha.

When he arrived at the place of execution, the cross was hoisted up and Jesus was crucified, along with two other criminals.

THE DEATH OF THE CHRIST

After a few hours of suffering, Jesus died.

Jesus' body was then taken down from the cross and a soldier pierced his right side with his spear to ensure his death.

Mary, the mother of Jesus, wept when she saw her dead son. John was also there.

Pontius Pilate had the letters "INRI" inscribed on Jesus' cross.

This means "Iesus Nazarenus Rex Iudaeorum", that is "Jesus the Nazarene, King of the Jews".

THE TOMB OF JESUS

Jesus was then wrapped in a shroud and placed in a tomb (also called a sepulchre) with the precious help of Joseph of Arimathea, a prominent Jew.

The entrance to the tomb was closed with a large stone.

Guards were posted next to the tomb to prevent the body from being stolen.

THE RESURRECTION OF JESUS

The following Sunday, Mary Magdalene and other women went to the tomb.

When they arrived, an angel appeared and moved the stone and sat on it.

The guards were so frightened that they fled. The angel said, "Jesus is not here because he has risen."

The women then rushed to tell the other disciples the news.

On the way, Jesus appeared and greeted them. The women fell down at his feet. Jesus said to them, "Go and tell my brothers and sisters that they must go to Galilee, for there they will see me."

JESUS ASCENDS TO HEAVEN

During the next forty days, Jesus appeared several times to his apostles and disciples. On one day, he even appeared to 500 people at the same time.

On the last day, Jesus commanded his disciples to travel the world and bring the Word of God.

Then he ascended into heaven.

It is said that one day Jesus will return to earth, and on that day the trumpets of God will sound in heaven. On that day, the earth will be transformed into paradise, without war, without disease, and even death will no longer exist.

Made in the USA
Columbia, SC
15 April 2025

56647503R20043